Note to Parents and Teachers

The READING ABOUT: STARTERS series introduces key science vocabulary to young children while encouraging them to discover and understand the world around them. The series works as a set of graded readers in three levels.

LEVEL 1: BEGINNING TO READ follows guidelines set out in the National Curriculum for Year 1. These books can be read alone or as part of guided or group reading. Each book has three sections:

• Information pages that introduce new words. These key words appear in bold throughout the book for easy recognition.
• A lively story that recalls this vocabulary and encourages children to use these words when they talk and write.
• A quiz and word search ask children to look back and recall what they have read.

ABOUT ME looks at THE HUMAN BODY. Below are some activities related to the questions on the information spreads that parents, carers and teachers can use to discuss and develop further ideas and concepts:

p. 5 *Do you have two of any other parts of your body?* You can ask children to identify and locate different parts of their body, perhaps by playing the game "Simon says".

p. 7 *Which parts of your body can you bend?* Exploring joints, e.g. elbows, knees.

p. 9 *Which food do you like best?* Exploring preferences. Ask children to think about what it is they like – e.g. smell, taste, how it feels (crunchy!), colour etc.

p. 11 *Are these foods sweet or sour? Which do you like?* Exploring tastes. You could do a blindfold "taste test" to see what flavours children can recognise.

p. 13 *Are all eyes the same colour?* Looking at differences/similarities in our bodies.

p. 15 *Put a hand behind your ear. Do you hear better?* Ask children to try this. Extend the discussion by asking children to think about which animals have big ears and why.

p. 17 *Have a good sniff. What can you smell?* Exploring different smells around us.

p. 19 *Why should you not touch very hot things?* Looking at safety issues around hot surfaces and liquids. Could also ask what else they shouldn't touch, e.g. stinging nettles.

p. 21 *How else can you keep clean?* Exploring personal hygiene issues.

p. 23 *Why do you need to sleep?* Ask children to think about what makes them tired.

ADVISORY TEAM

Educational Consultant
Andrea Bright – Science Co-ordinator, Trafalgar Junior School, Twickenham

Literacy Consultant
Jackie Holderness – former Senior Lecturer in Primary Education, Westminster Institute, Oxford Brookes University

Series Consultants
Anne Fussell – Early Years Teacher and University Tutor, Westminster College, Oxford Brookes University

David Fussell – C.Chem., FRSC

CONTENTS

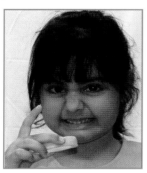

© Aladdin Books Ltd 2004

Designed and produced by
Aladdin Books Ltd
2/3 Fitzroy Mews
London W1T 6DF

First published in
Great Britain in 2004 by
Franklin Watts
96 Leonard Street
London EC2A 4XD

A catalogue record for this
book is available from the
British Library.

ISBN 0 7496 5589 5

Printed in UAE

All rights reserved

Editor: Jim Pipe

Design: Flick, Book Design
and Graphics

Picture research:
Brian Hunter Smart

Thanks to:
• The pupils of Trafalgar Infants
School, Twickenham for
appearing as models in this book.
• Lynne Thompson for helping to
organise the photoshoots.
• The pupils and teachers of
Trafalgar Junior School,
Twickenham and St. Nicholas
C.E. Infant School, Wallingford,
for testing the sample books.

Photocredits:
l-left, r-right, b-bottom, t-top,
c-centre, m-middle
Front cover tl, 2mlb, 6, 7b, 8, 12,
23, 32tr, 32br — Brand X Pictures.
Front cover tm & tr, 2mlt, 5, 9tr,
10tr, 11c, 13 both, 14br, 16, 17,
21, 22, 24br, 27b, 28tl, 28bl,
31ml, 31mr, 31bl, 32tl, 32mlt,
32mlc, 32mlb, 32mrt, 32mrc —
PBD. Front cover b, 2tl, 10b, 18 —
Photodisc. 3, 7tr, 19 both, 26tr,
31tr, 32mrb — Corbis. 4, 29ml —
Comstock. 9b, 30tl — Digital
Vision. 11ml, 11bl, 11mr, 11br —
Stockbyte. 14t — John Foxx
Images. 15 — Corel. 20, 29br,
32mrc, 32bl — Jim Pipe. 24 both,
25tl 26bl, 27tl, 28mr, 29tr, 30mr
— Flick Smith.

612

READING ABOUT

Starters

HUMAN BODY

About Me

by Sally Hewitt

Aladdin/Watts

London • Sydney

I have a **body**.

My dog has a **body** too.

He has a tail, but I do not!

My head is on top of my **body**.
I have two arms,
two legs,
two hands and
two feet.

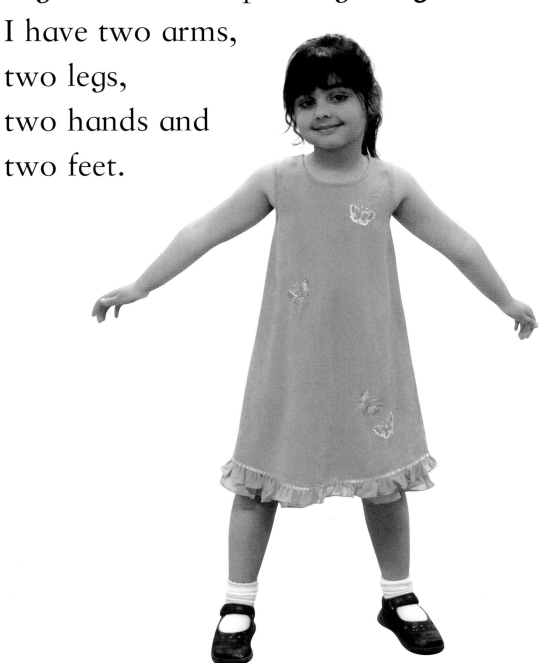

• Do you have two of any other parts of your body?

I can run and jump.
I can kick a ball.

When I **move**, **muscles** pull my bones.

When I smile,
muscles move my face.

When I write, **muscles move** my fingers.

• Which parts of your body can you bend?

I eat food every day.

Good food gives me strength
to grow, work and play.

I open my **mouth** and put in my food.

I chew it up with my **teeth**. Then I swallow it. Yummy!

• Which food do you like best?

This is my **tongue**.

When I lick food,
I can **taste** it with
my **tongue**.

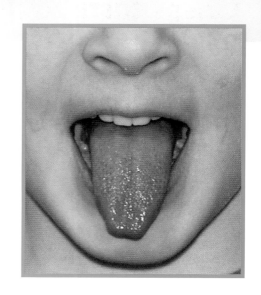

I like the **taste** of a biscuit.
A biscuit **tastes** sweet.

Crisps **taste** salty.
A lemon **tastes** sour.
There are lots of **tastes**.

Cheese

Crisps

Pear

Orange

Lemon

• Are these foods sweet or sour? Which do you like?

When my **eyes** are open

I can **see** colours.

I can **see** shapes.

I can **see** things moving.

12

You **see** when light goes into your **eyes**.

Look around you.
What can you **see** now?

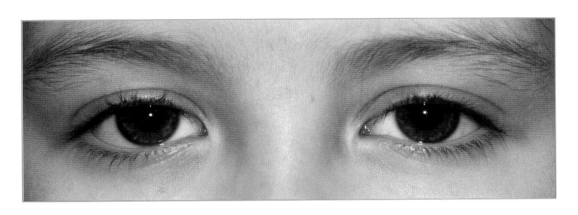

When you shut your **eyes**
you cannot **see**!

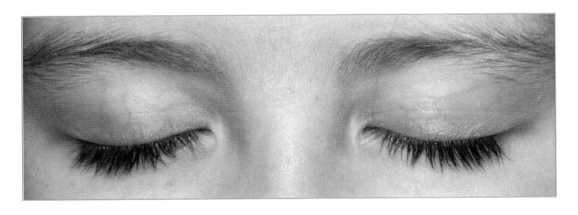

• Are all eyes the same colour?

When I listen with my **ears**
I can **hear** loud **sounds**.
I can **hear** a telephone.
I can **hear** a dog barking.

14

I can **hear** soft **sounds** too.
I can **hear** whispering
and a cat purring.

• Put a hand behind your ear. Do you hear better?

When I sniff with my **nose**
I can **smell** things.
Some **smells** are nice.
Some **smells** are nasty!

I have two holes in my **nose**.
They are called **nostrils**.
Smells go up my **nostrils** when I sniff.

• *Have a good sniff. What can you smell?*

I **feel** with my **skin**.
My guinea pig **feels** with its whiskers.

Some things **feel** soft.
Some things hurt my **skin**!

18

My **skin feels** cold after a swim.

My **skin feels** warm when I am wrapped in a soft towel.

• Why should you not touch very hot things?

I **wash** my hands before I eat.
Washing my hands gets rid of **germs**.

Germs can make me ill.

I **brush** my teeth after I eat.

Brushing my teeth gets rid of **germs**.
It keeps my teeth strong and healthy.

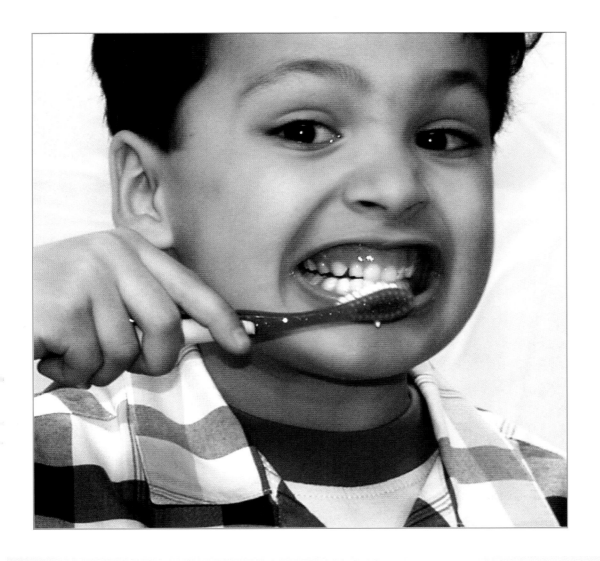

• How else can you keep clean?

What a busy day!
Now I feel **tired**.
I yawn when I am **tired**.

It is my bedtime.

I get into bed and go to **sleep**.

Sometimes I dream.

• Why do you need to sleep?

Now read the story of
The Lost Ball.
Look out for words
about your **body**.

I am playing ball
with Scruff.
I throw the ball and
Scruff fetches it.

Scruff has four legs.
He can **move** faster than I can.
I have only two legs.

Oh no!
The ball has
landed in the bush!

We can't **see** it.

Scruff is clever.
He can find the ball
with his **nose**.

He **smells** the ball.

I can **smell**
something with
my **nose** too.

It isn't the ball –
it's something
yummy!

It's dinner!

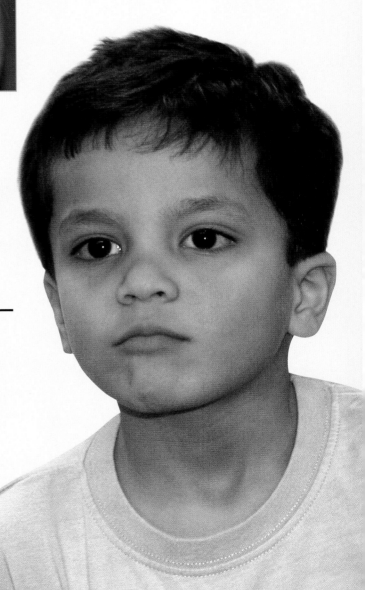

It's pasta for dinner.
I love the **smell**
of pasta sauce.

I love the **taste**
too. I lick it up
with my **tongue**.

Scruff likes to
lick his bowl
with his **tongue**.

But where is
Scruff?
Scruff! Scruff!
Where are you?

I listen, but I can't **hear** Scruff barking. I can't **hear** him running around.

I put my hand behind my **ear**. I still can't **hear** him!

I look under the table.
I look behind the door.
I look everywhere but
I can't **see** him.

I cry, "Scruff is lost!"
I wipe tears out of my **eyes**.

There's Scruff!
He's covered in
twigs and leaves.
He's found the ball.

I say, "Good
boy, Scruff!"

28

Scruff licks me
with his **tongue**.
It **feels** wet
on my **skin**.
His **nose feels** cold.

I stroke his soft fur.

Scruff's coat needs a
brush. My hands and
face need a **wash**.

Now we are both clean!

What a long day!
Scruff and I are **tired**.

I fall fast **asleep**...
and so does Scruff.

Draw a picture of
your **body**.
Write a label to
show each part.

Don't forget
your **eyes**, **ears**,
nose and **mouth**!

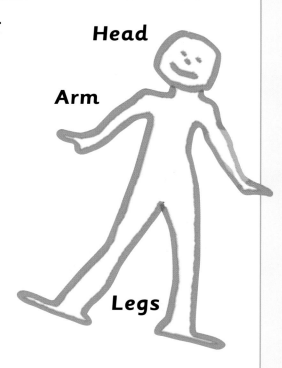

Head

Arm

Legs

QUIZ

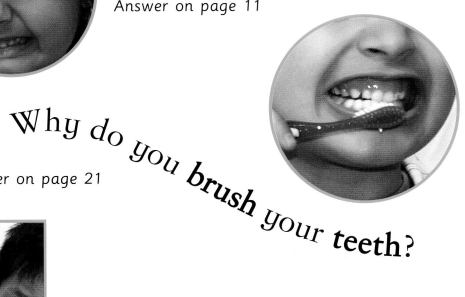

What **moves** your face when you smile?

Answer on page 7

What **tastes** sour?

Answer on page 11

Why do you **brush** your **teeth**?

Answer on page 21

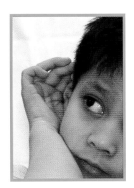

What do you **hear** with?

Answer on page 14

Did you know the answers? Give yourself a

Do you remember these **body** words?
Well done! Can you remember any more?

 **body**
page 5

muscles
page 6

 **mouth**
page 9

tongue
page 10
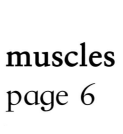

 **eyes**
page 13

ears
page 14
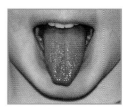

 **nose**
page 17

skin
page 19

 **wash**
page 20

sleep
page 23